Hall and West Door. Buff Walls, Light Grey Woodwork—1797

SWEETBRIER, FAIRMOUNT PARK, PHILADELPHIA

COLONIAL INTERIORS

FEDERAL AND GREEK REVIVAL

THIRD SERIES

BY

HAROLD DONALDSON EBERLEIN

AND

CORTLANDT VAN DYKE HUBBARD

19 38

WILLIAM HELBURN INC

15 EAST 55TH ST NEW YORK, N.Y.

To

JEFFERSON GIBBON EBERLEIN

Whose continued and whole-hearted
interest in their work the authors
gratefully acknowledge

FOREWORD

N THIS third series of domestic interiors and interior details, the territory covered for material differs altogether from that represented in the two preceding volumes. The first, by Leigh French, junior, dealt entirely with New England, chiefly Connecticut. The second, by Mrs. Edith Tunis Sale, confined its scope to the South, or rather parts of the South; Mrs. Sale gathered her material almost wholly from Virginia, with a few examples from Maryland and South Carolina.

For the present volume, the authors have drawn upon the rich field afforded by southeastern Pennsylvania, the Jerseys and Delaware, and have also taken a few instances from New York, New Hampshire and Maryland. Most of the Pennsylvania material is either from Philadelphia or from nearby parts of the State.

In another respect, too, this third volume differs from its two predecessors. Both the first and second volumes showed almost exclusively examples well within the Colonial period or else dating from the immediately post-Revolutionary era. Indeed, most of the emphasis fell on the middle-Georgian phase of domestic architecture, while the early and late Georgian examples held a subsidiary position.

Although not neglecting the middle-Georgian episode—it was, in many ways, the Golden Age of eighteenth-century building in the American Colonies—the authors have endeavoured to give more adequate consideration to both the earlier and later Georgian modes. They have made special efforts to invite attention—now more generally favourable than heretofore—to the many excellences of the Regency or Federal manner that commend it to contemporary regard.

In arranging the illustrations—both those showing general composition and those devoted to some special feature, such as windows or doorways—it has seemed desirable to follow a chronological sequence indicative of the course of historical development. At the same time, it is well to remember that the course of changes in style expression was very considerably affected by locality and by the greater or less conservatism of individual craftsmen and designers. As an instance of such conservatism affecting design, there is the Bartram house, at Kingsessing, Philadelphia. Although the later portion dates from 1770, the personal tastes of John Bartram—who built the house with his own hands—

dictated adherence to forms earlier than the date itself would lead us to expect. Other houses in the neighbourhood of Philadelphia, with which Bartram could scarcely have been unfamiliar, exhibited a distinct change of style that immediately preceded the post-Revolutionary outburst of Neo-Classic elegance; nevertheless, the Quaker botanist held to the architectural type in vogue nearly fifty years before.

Where houses were built at two or more successive dates, all the dates are given in the legends, and the date to which the particular part illustrated belongs is given in parenthesis. For instance, Andalusia in its present form is the result of three main activities of building. Of the original structure little visible trace remains; the rooms or features illustrated belong either to 1795 or to 1830, and are so indicated in the accompanying parentheses. Again, when two dates are close together, as in the case of the Read House at New Castle, it means that the house was two or three years in building.

In many cases, the photographs were taken with a six-foot rule conspicuously exposed, so that both the scale and the general characteristics of the details may be visible at one and the same time, in each case. Wherever they may be of either use or interest, notes appear in the legends regarding the colours of woodwork, walls, floors and the like, and of the principal features in the movable appointments. No notice is taken, however, where the colouring is of purely present devising as, for example, at Laurel Lodge, Pottstown—a fine old house now used as a civic centre and painted any colour inside that happened to suit the convenience of the moment.

The authors take this occasion to express their sincere thanks to all who have assisted in the preparation of this book by their permission to take photographs, to obtain measurements and data, and by their many courtesies extended in sundry ways; especially do they wish to acknowledge their indebtedness to Mrs. J. Amory Haskell, Mrs. John Henry Livingston, Mrs. Henry Flather, Miss Caroline Sinkler, Miss Frances A. Wister, Miss Sarah Lowrey, the Reverend and Mrs. Caleb Cresson, 5th, Mr. and Mrs. Philip Dandridge Laird, Mr. and Mrs. Charles J. Biddle, Eli Kirk Price, 3rd, Esq., Henry N. Woolman, Esq., D. T. V. Huntoon, Esq., William Wayne, Esq., the John Bartram Association and the Philadelphia Park Commission. Likewise, they desire to record their particular obligations to Clifford Lewis, junior, Esq., of the Mutual Assurance Company for Insuring Houses from Loss by Fire, and to Sydney E. Martin, Esq., of the Philadelphia Chapter of the American Institute of Architects, for permission to reproduce measured drawings; also to the Thomas Jefferson Memorial Association for permission to use several illustrations from Monticello.

Philadelphia, November, 1937

HAROLD DONALDSON EBERLEIN
CORTLANDT VAN DYKE HUBBARD

TABLE OF PLATES
COLONIAL INTERIORS, THIRD SERIES

TABLE OF PLATES

TABLE OF PLATES

STAIRS AND STAIR DETAILS

PARLOURS, LIVING ROOMS AND LIBRARIES

TABLE OF PLATES

DINING ROOMS

TABLE OF PLATES

TABLE OF PLATES

TABLE OF PLATES

TABLE OF PLATES

PLATE 1

COLONIAL INTERIORS, THIRD SERIES

South Door—c. 1735, 1780, c. 1830

CARLTON, GERMANTOWN, PHILADELPHIA

Hall Door—1684, c. 1710-1730

MARLPIT HALL, MIDDLETOWN, NEW JERSEY

PLATE 2

COLONIAL INTERIORS, THIRD SERIES

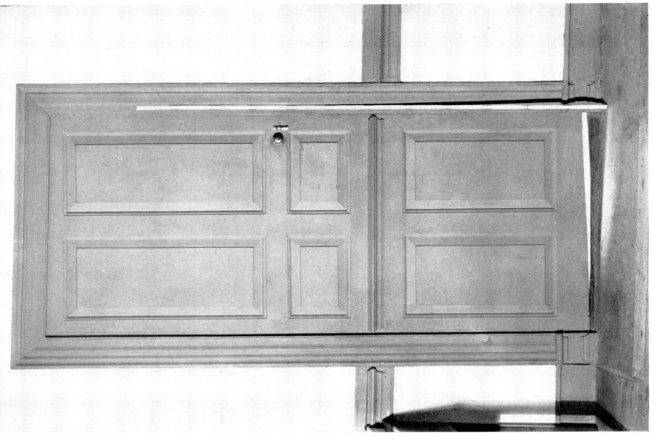

Hall, Door Detail—1684, c. 1710-1730

MARLPIT HALL, MIDDLETOWN, NEW JERSEY

Hall, Details—1756

WOODFORD, FAIRMOUNT PARK, PHILADELPHIA

PLATE 3

COLONIAL INTERIORS, THIRD SERIES

Door from Lower Hall to Portico—1731, 1770

BARTRAM HOUSE, BARTRAM'S
GARDEN, KINGSESSING,
PHILADELPHIA

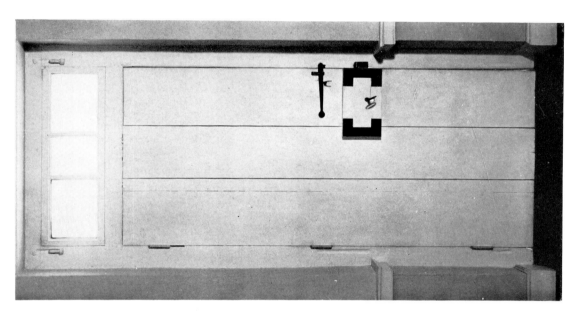

Outside Door with Wooden Box Lock—1750

THE INDIAN KING, HADDONFIELD,
NEW JERSEY

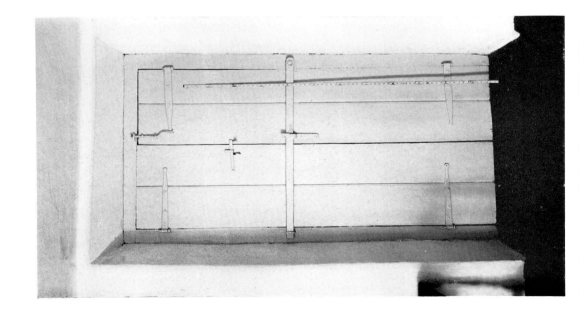

House Door—c. 1765

WASHINGTON'S HEADQUARTERS,
VALLEY FORGE, PENNSYLVANIA

PLATE 4

COLONIAL INTERIORS, THIRD SERIES

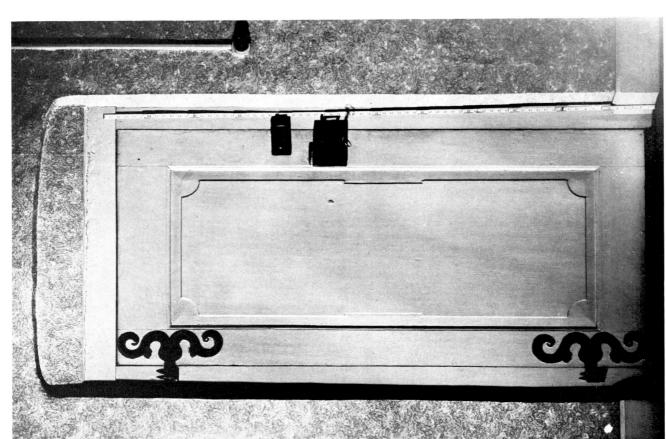

Door in room on upper floor—1742

Door in room on ground floor—1742.

MORAVIAN *GEMEINHAUS*, BETHLEHEM, PENNSYLVANIA

PLATE 5

COLONIAL INTERIORS, THIRD SERIES

House Door—1765

POWEL HOUSE, 244, SOUTH 3RD ST.,
PHILADELPHIA

Door in Hall. Woodwork grey; walls white—c. 1740

TEUNIS DEY HOUSE, PREAKNESS,
NEW JERSEY

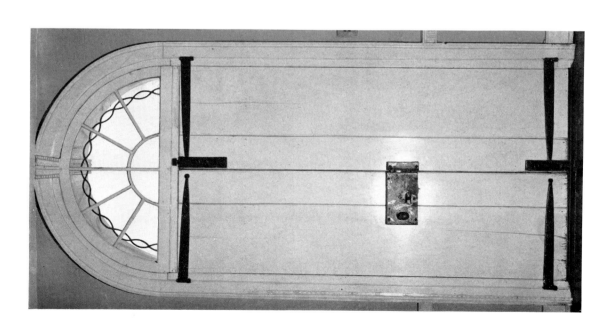

House Door—c. 1730, c. 1770

PINE FORGE HOUSE, PINE FORGE,
PENNSYLVANIA

PLATE 6

COLONIAL INTERIORS, THIRD SERIES

Parlour, Door Detail—1765

POWEL HOUSE, 244, SOUTH 3RD ST., PHILADELPHIA

Door in Oval Drawing Room (now Dining Room)—c. 1742, 1788

THE WOODLANDS, BLOCKLEY, PHILADELPHIA

Doorhead in Parlour, Added by Chancellor Livingston—(c. 1800), 1730, 1778, c. 1810

CLERMONT, LIVINGSTON MANOR, TVOLI-ON-HUDSON, NEW YORK

Doorhead in Parlour—c. 1742, 1788

THE WOODLANDS, BLOCKLEY, PHILADELPHIA

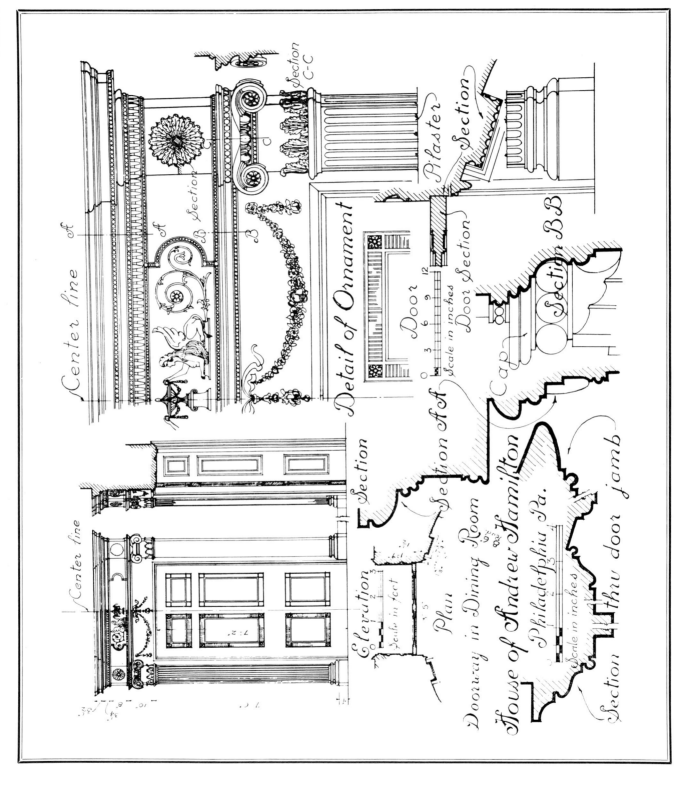

PLATE 8

Center line of

Center line of

A

A

B Section

B

Section C-C

Pilaster

Section

Detail of Ornament

Door

Scale in inches

Door Section

Cap

Section BB

Center line

Elevation

Scale in feet

Plan

Section

Section of A

Doorway in Dining Room

House of Andrew Hamilton

Philadelphia, Pa.

Scale in inches

Section thru door jamb

PLATE 9

COLONIAL INTERIORS, THIRD SERIES

Same door in adjacent room, with different detail of trim—1798-1801

READ HOUSE, NEW CASTLE, DELAWARE

Door in Bedroom—1798-1801.

PLATE 10

COLONIAL INTERIORS, THIRD SERIES

Door in Library—c. 1815

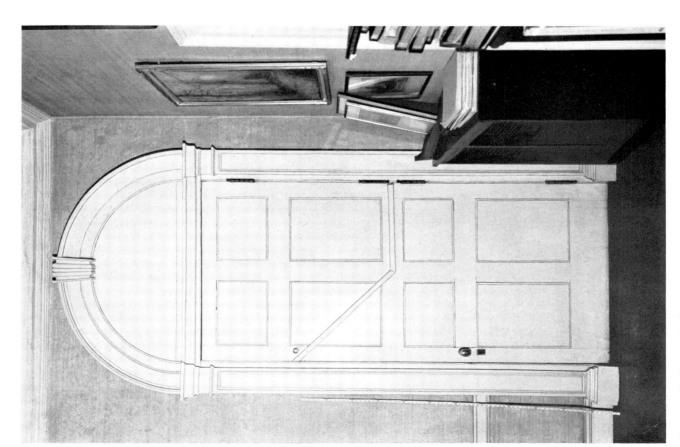

Door in Hall—c. 1815.

ROXBOROUGH, SCHOOL LANE, GERMANTOWN, PHILADELPHIA

Hall Door—1812

GEORGE B. HOLLAND HOUSE, WALPOLE, NEW HAMPSHIRE

PLATE 12

COLONIAL INTERIORS, THIRD SERIES

Dining Room. Doorway Detail (c. 1800)—1730, 1778, c. 1810

CLERMONT, LIVINGSTON MANOR
TIVOLI-ON-HUDSON, NEW YORK

Parlour, Door Detail—c. 1818

HOUSE IN CASTLETON, VERMONT

PLATE 13

COLONIAL INTERIORS, THIRD SERIES

Door between Parlours. White woodwork; Panels in grisaille and gold; relief ornament over door painted in bronze—1826
CADWALADER HOUSE (Mutual Assurance Co.), 240, SOUTH 4TH ST., PHILADELPHIA

Door in Parlour—1730, 1778, c. 1810. (Door Trim of c. 1810)
CLERMONT, LIVINGSTON MANOR
TIVOLI-ON-HUDSON, NEW YORK

PLATE 14

COLONIAL INTERIORS, THIRD SERIES

Door in Parlour; Relief decorations on doorhead in bronze paint

Details of panel decorations in grisaille and gold—1826.

CADWALADER HOUSE (Mutual Assurance Co.), 240, SOUTH 4TH ST., PHILADELPHIA

PLATE 15

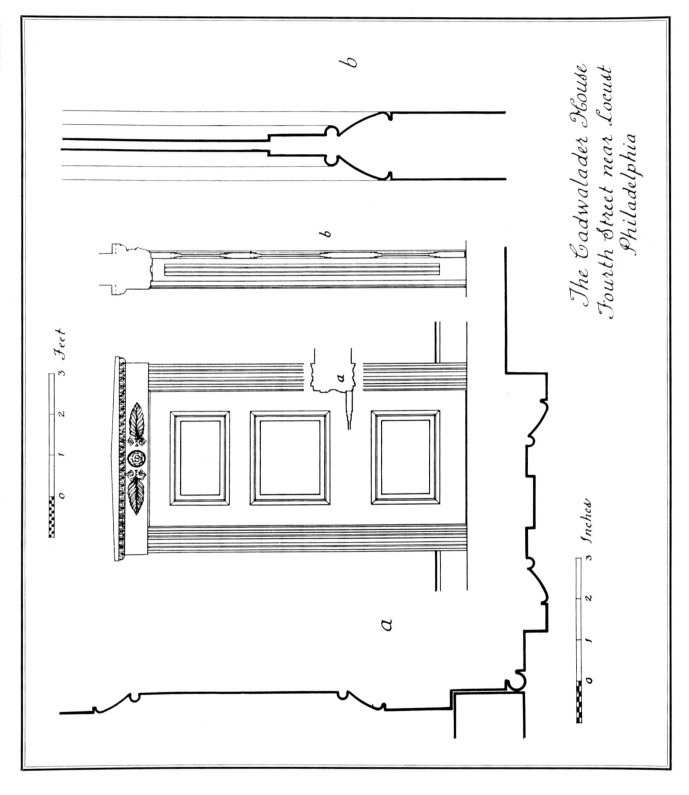

The Cadwalader House
Fourth Street near Locust
Philadelphia

PLATE 16

COLONIAL INTERIORS, THIRD SERIES

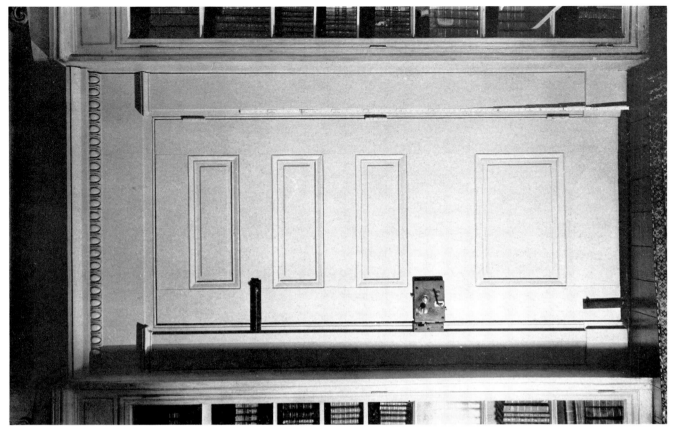

West Door in Library (1830)—c. 1750, 1795, 1830
ANDALUSIA, PENNSYLVANIA

*Door in South Parlour. Walls pearl lavender. Door trim white. Stiles and
rails of door pearl lavender, mouldings white, fields of panels light blue—1836*
OAKLAND HALL, OAKS, PENNSYLVANIA

PLATE 17

COLONIAL INTERIORS, THIRD SERIES

Door in Parlour. Stiles and rails light chocolate brown; mouldings white, panels salmon—1760, 1835

HATFIELD HOUSE, FAIRMOUNT PARK, PHILADELPHIA

Doorway in Hall—c. 1756, c. 1787, 1832

MASTER'S HOUSE, ELIZABETH FURNACE, PENNSYLVANIA

Circular Vestibule—c. 1742, 1788

THE WOODLANDS, BLOCKLEY, PHILADELPHIA

PLATE 19

COLONIAL INTERIORS, THIRD SERIES

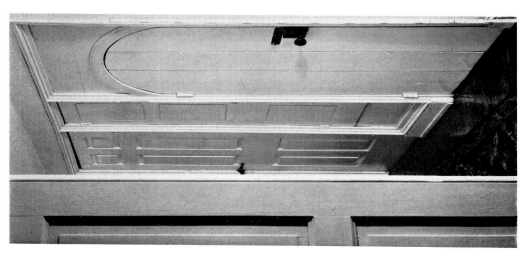

Doors in Upstairs Cross Hall—c. 1742, 1788

THE WOODLANDS, BLOCKLEY, PHILADELPHIA

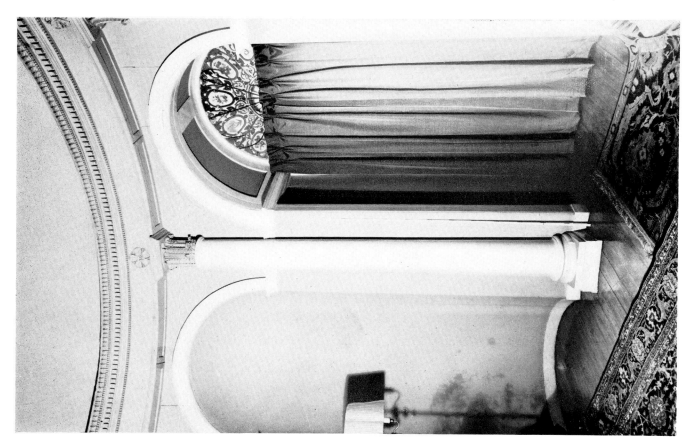

Detail of Circular Vestibule—c. 1742, 1788

THE WOODLANDS, BLOCKLEY PHILADELPHIA

Detail of Woodwork in Hall—1798-1801

UPSALA, GERMANTOWN, PHILADELPHIA

PLATE 20

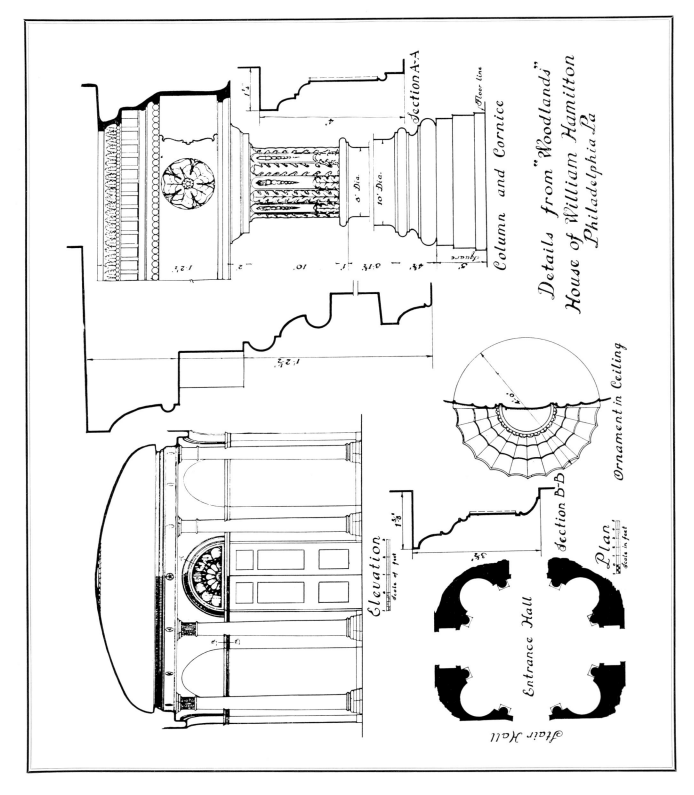

Column and Cornice

Details from "Woodlands"
House of William Hamilton
Philadelphia Pa

Ornament in Ceiling

Elevation

Section B-B

Plan

Entrance Hall

Stair Hall

Door in Vestibule. Walls pearl lavender. Stiles and rails of door pearl lavender, mouldings white, panels light blue. On floor, original floriated and foliated polychrome oilcloth, at the period the fashionable alternative to marble tiles—1836

OAKLAND HALL, OAKS, PENNSYLVANIA

Door in Vestibule—1826

CADWALADER HOUSE (Mutual Assurance Co.), 240, SOUTH 4TH ST., PHILADELPHIA

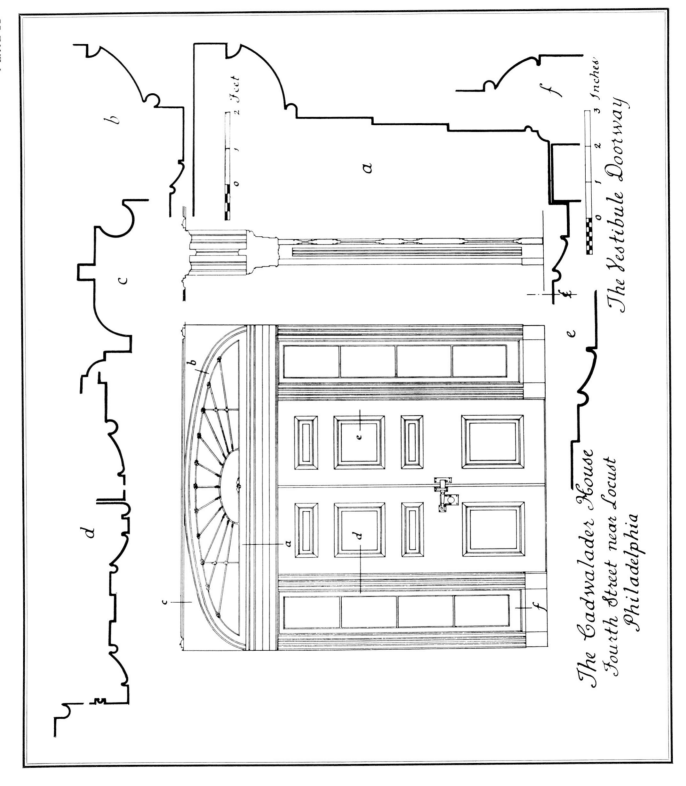

The Cadwalader House
Fourth Street near Locust
Philadelphia

The Vestibule Doorway

PLATE 23

COLONIAL INTERIORS, THIRD SERIES

Hall and Stair. Woodwork sage green, walls white—1684, c. 1710-1730

MARLPIT HALL, MIDDLETOWN, NEW JERSEY

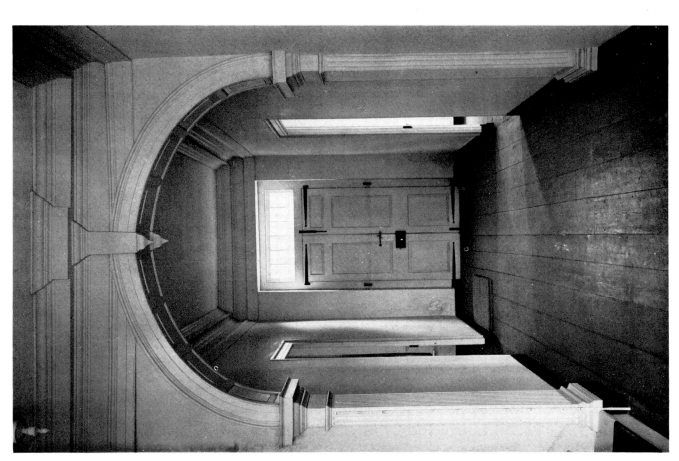

Hall. Woodwork white; walls white—1719

TRENT HOUSE, TRENTON, NEW JERSEY

Upper Hall—1731, 1770

BARTRAM HOUSE, BARTRAM'S GARDEN, KINGSESSING, PHILADELPHIA

Lower Hall and Stair—1731, 1770

BARTRAM HOUSE, BARTRAM'S GARDEN, KINGSESSING, PHILADELPHIA

Hall and South Door—c. 1730, c. 1770

PINE FORGE HOUSE, PINE FORGE, PENNSYLVANIA

Hall, Stair and North Door—c. 1730, c. 1770

PINE FORGE HOUSE, PINE FORGE, PENNSYLVANIA

PLATE 27

COLONIAL INTERIORS, THIRD SERIES

Hall (1795). Woodwork white, walls pale green—c. 1750, 1795, 1830

ANDALUSIA, PENNSYLVANIA

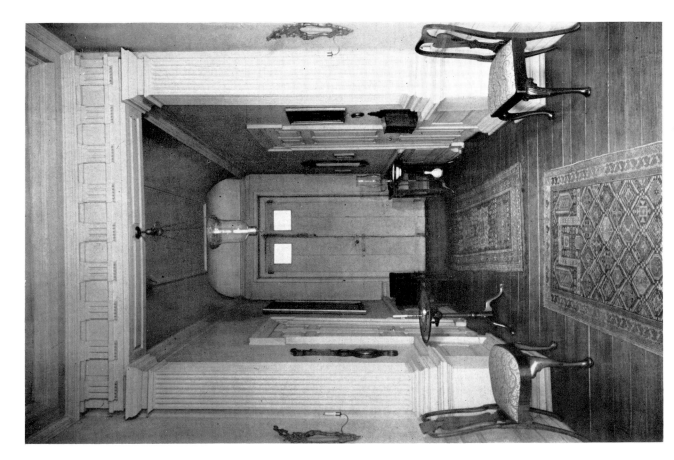

Hall. Woodwork white, walls pale primrose yellow—1756

WOODFORD, FAIRMOUNT PARK, PHILADELPHIA

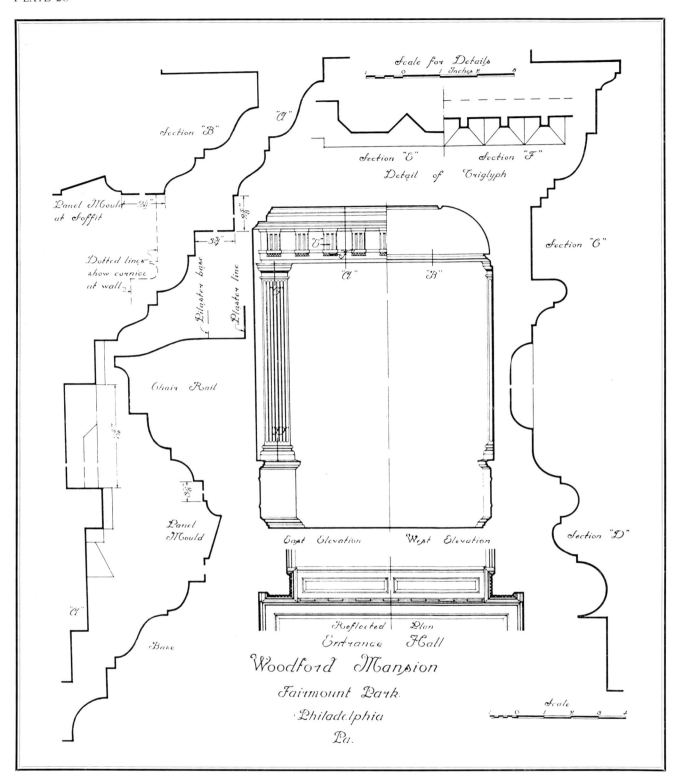

Scale for Details

Section "B"

"A"

Section "E"   Section "F"

Detail of Triglyph

Panel Mould 2½"
at Soffit

Section "C"

Dotted lines
show cornice
at wall

Plaster base

Plaster line

"E"

"A"   "B"

Chair Rail

Section "D"

Panel
Mould

East Elevation   West Elevation

"A"

Base   Reflected   Plan
                      Entrance   Hall

Woodford Mansion

Fairmount Park

Philadelphia

Pa.

Scale

PLATE 29

COLONIAL INTERIORS, THIRD SERIES

Hall and Stair—1765

POWEL HOUSE, 244, SOUTH 3RD ST., PHILADELPHIA

Stair Detail—1765.

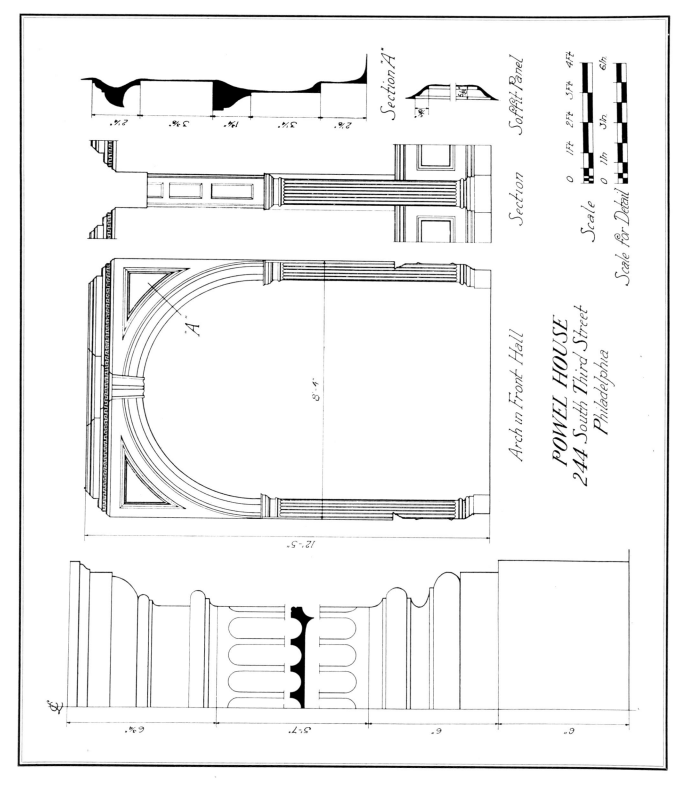

Section "A"

Section   Soffit Panel

Arch in Front Hall

POWEL HOUSE
244 South Third Street
Philadelphia

Scale

0 1Ft 2Ft 3Ft 4Ft

0 1In. 3In. 6In.

Scale for Detail

PLATE 31

COLONIAL INTERIORS, THIRD SERIES

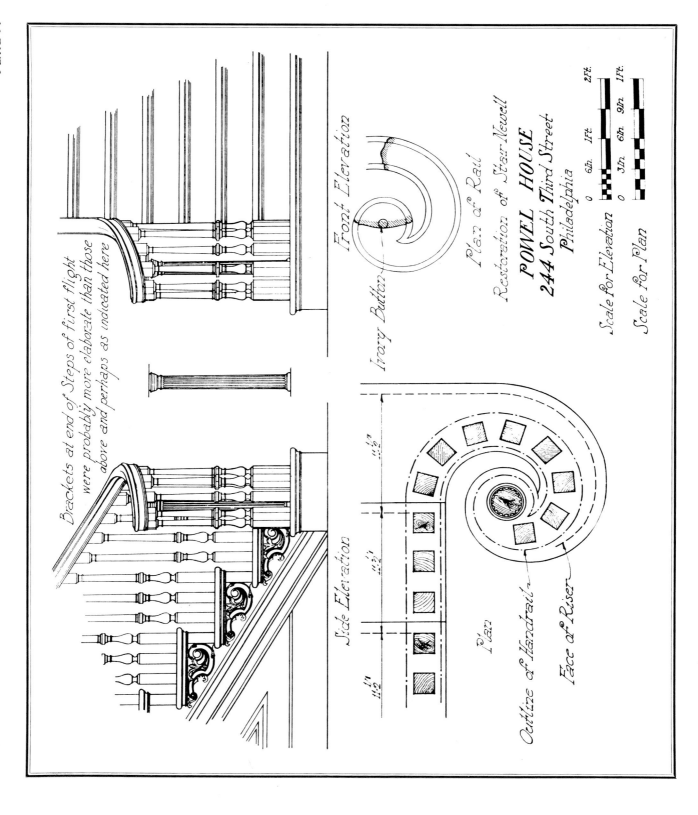

Brackets at end of Steps of first flight
were probably more elaborate than those
above and perhaps as indicated here

Side Elevation

Front Elevation

Ivory Button

Plan of Rail

Restoration of Stair-Newell

POWEL HOUSE
244 South Third Street
Philadelphia

Scale for Elevation

Scale for Plan

Plan

Outline of Handrail

Face of Riser

Hall and Stair. Woodwork white; walls white; stair balustrade mahogany—1756

TULIP HILL, WEST RIVER, ANNE ARUNDEL COUNTY, MARYLAND

Main Hall. Polychrome landscape paper; woodwork white. Doorway at end, cornice and much of woodwork changed in 1830. Black and white chequerings of floor painted at later date—1796, 1830

THE HIGHLANDS, WHITEMARSH VALLEY, PENNSYLVANIA

PLATE 33

COLONIAL INTERIORS, THIRD SERIES

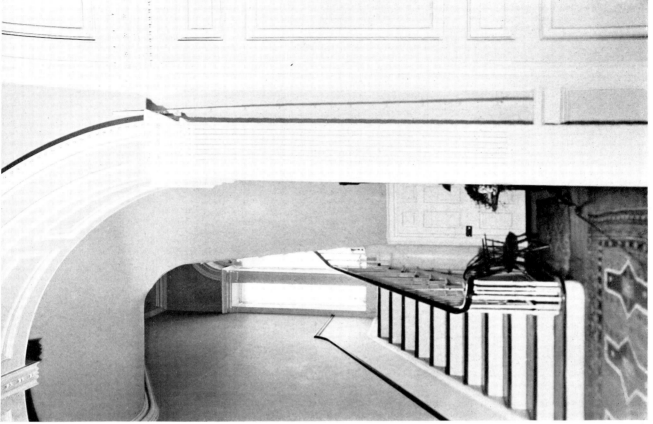

Stair Hall and Stair—1798-1801

READ HOUSE, NEW CASTLE, DELAWARE

Hall—1798-1801

READ HOUSE, NEW CASTLE, DELAWARE

Hall and Stair—1798-1801

UPSALA, GERMANTOWN, PHILADELPHIA

Stair and Archway Detail. Buff Walls, Light Grey Woodwork—1797

SWEETBRIER, FAIRMOUNT PARK, PHILADELPHIA

PLATE 36

COLONIAL INTERIORS, THIRD SERIES

Hall, Stair and North Door—c. 1735, 1780, c. 1830

CARLTON, GERMANTOWN, PHILADELPHIA

Stair Hall and Stair—1796, 1830. The floors of the stair hall and long hall,
at a later date, were painted in black and white chequers.

THE HIGHLANDS, WHITE MARSH VALLEY, PENNSYLVANIA

PLATE 37

COLONIAL INTERIORS, THIRD SERIES

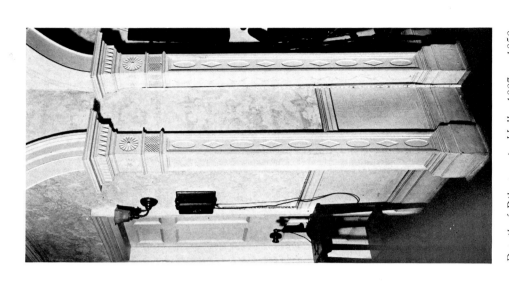

Detail of Pilasters in Hall—1807, c. 1850

AULD HOUSE, REDBANK,
NEW JERSEY (formerly on Long Island)

Upstairs Hall and Screen. Walls pale buff—1826

CADWALADER HOUSE (Mutual Assurance Co.), 240, SOUTH
4TH ST., PHILADELPHIA

*Detail of Arch in Hall—c. 1756, c. 1787,
c. 1832*

THE MASTER'S HOUSE,
ELIZABETH FURNACE,
PENNSYLVANIA

COLONIAL INTERIORS, THIRD SERIES

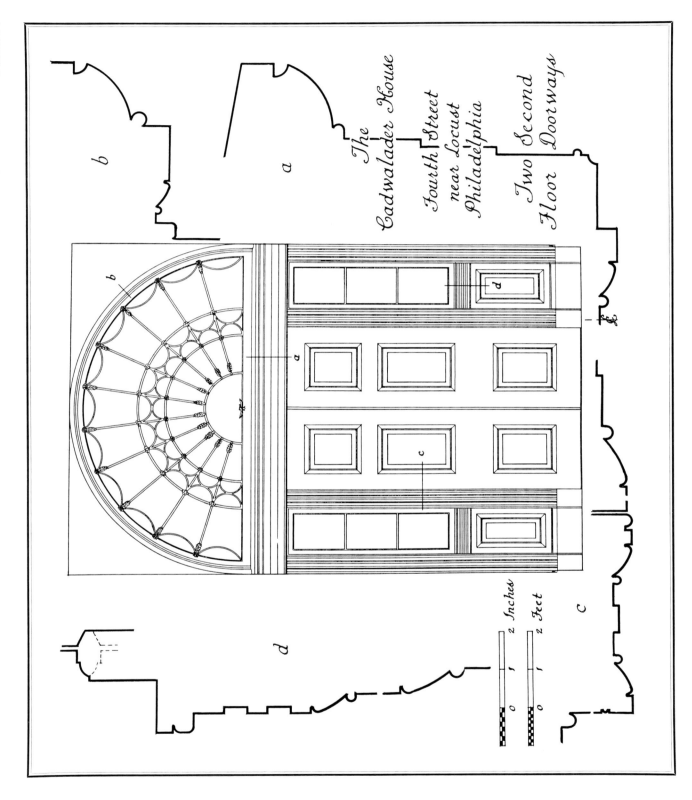

PLATE 38

The
Cadwalader House
Fourth Street
near Locust
Philadelphia

Two Second
Floor Doorways

2 Inches

2 Feet

PLATE 39

COLONIAL INTERIORS, THIRD SERIES

Lower Hall and Stair—1826

CADWALADER HOUSE (Mutual Assurance Co.), 240, SOUTH 4TH ST., PHILADELPHIA

PLATE 40

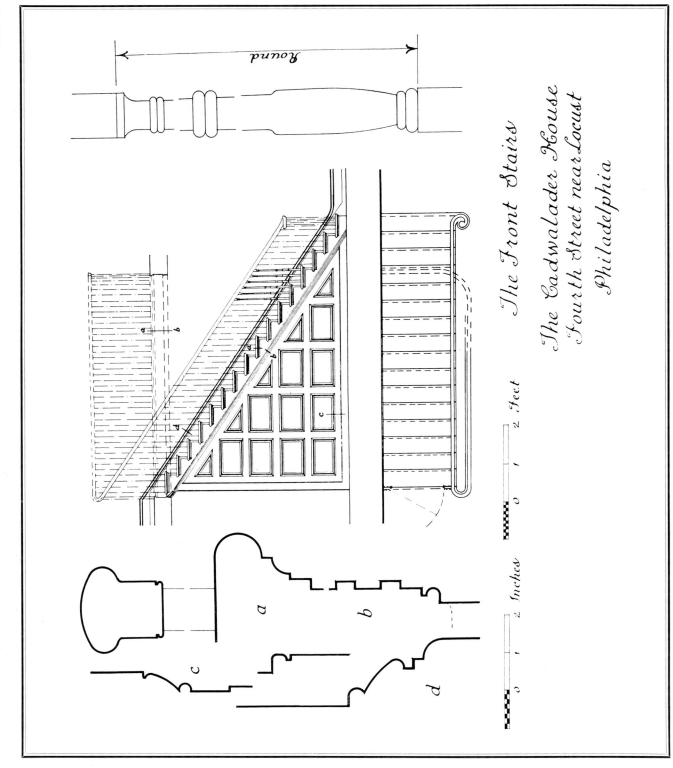

Round

The Front Stairs

The Cadwalader House
Fourth Street near Locust
Philadelphia

Inches

Feet

PLATE 41

COLONIAL INTERIORS, THIRD SERIES

Stair Detail—c. 1690, c. 1725, c. 1830

SUNBURY HOUSE, CROYDON, BUCKS, PENNSYLVANIA

Stair and Stair Cupboard—c. 1690, c. 1725, c. 1830

SUNBURY HOUSE, CROYDON, BUCKS, PENNSYLVANIA

PLATE 42

COLONIAL INTERIORS, THIRD SERIES

Hall and Stair—1719

Detail of Stair—1719

TRENT HOUSE, TRENTON, NEW JERSEY

PLATE 43

COLONIAL INTERIORS, THIRD SERIES

Detail, Bottom of Stair—1731, 1770

Top of Stair from ground floor—1731, 1770

BARTRAM HOUSE, KINGSESSING, PHILADELPHIA

PLATE 44

COLONIAL INTERIORS, THIRD SERIES

Stair and Panelling Details—1730

TYLER HOUSE, HANCOCK'S BRIDGE, SALEM COUNTY,
NEW JERSEY

Stair Details—1734

HANCOCK HOUSE, HANCOCK'S BRIDGE, SALEM COUNTY,
NEW JERSEY

PLATE 45

COLONIAL INTERIORS, THIRD SERIES

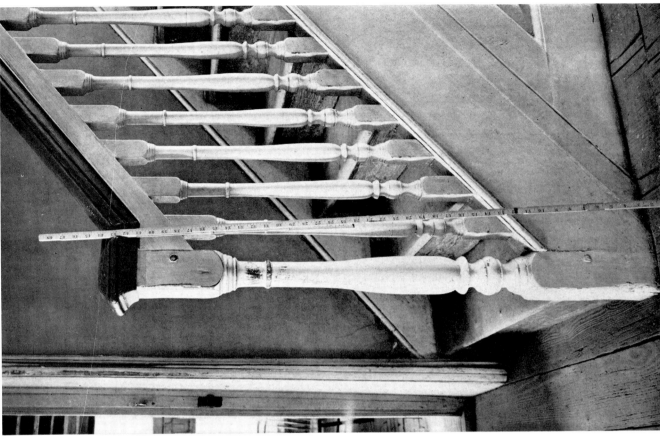

Stair Detail—c. 1765

WASHINGTON'S HEADQUARTERS, VALLEY FORGE,
PENNSYLVANIA

Stair Detail—1765. Paint recent

LAUREL LODGE, POTTSTOWN, PENNSYLVANIA

PLATE 46

COLONIAL INTERIORS, THIRD SERIES

Hall and Stair. Red quarry tile floor—1742

MORAVIAN SISTERS' HOUSE, BETHLEHEM, PENNSYLVANIA

Stair Detail—1750

THE INDIAN KING, HADDONFIELD, NEW JERSEY

PLATE 47

COLONIAL INTERIORS, THIRD SERIES

Stair Hall and Stair. Woodwork white, walls pale yellow—1756

WOODFORD, FAIRMOUNT PARK, PHILADELPHIA

Detail of Stair—1756

PLATE 48

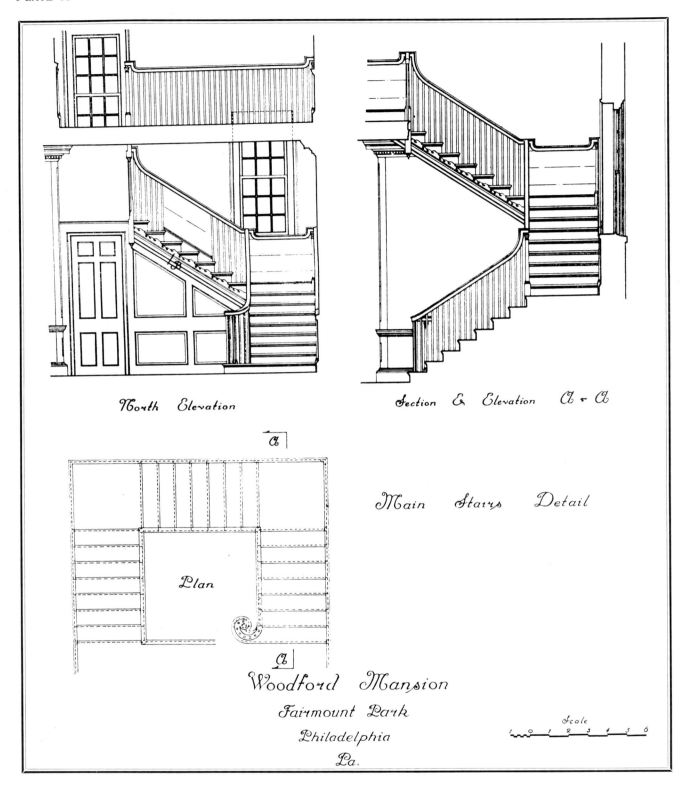

North Elevation

Section & Elevation A - A

Main Stairs Detail

Plan

Woodford Mansion

Fairmount Park

Philadelphia

Pa.

Scale

Stair Detail. Woodwork and walls white: Handrail and Spindles mahogany—1756   *Bottom of Stair and Newel Detail—1756*

TULIP HILL, WEST RIVER, ANNE ARUNDEL COUNTY, MARYLAND

PLATE 50

COLONIAL INTERIORS, THIRD SERIES

Hall and Stair—1750

THE INDIAN KING, HADDONFIELD, NEW JERSEY

Hall and Stair—1812

HOUSE IN COLUMBIA, LANCASTER CO., PENNSYLVANIA

PLATE 51

COLONIAL INTERIORS, THIRD SERIES

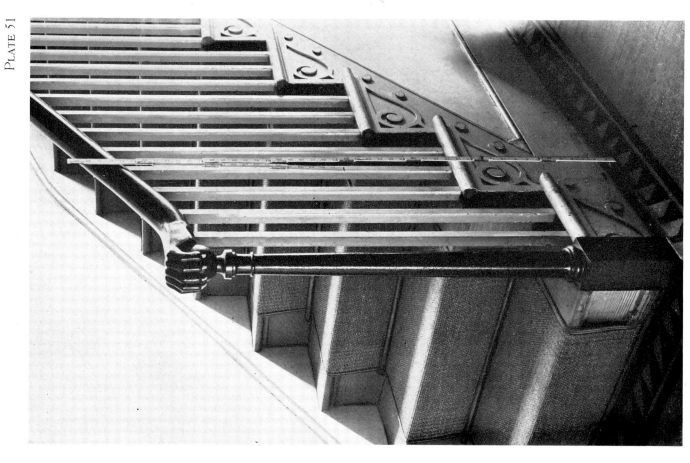

Stair Detail—1756, c. 1787, c. 1832

MASTER'S HOUSE, ELIZABETH FURNACE, PENNSYLVANIA

Stair Detail—1812

HOUSE IN COLUMBIA, LANCASTER CO., PENNSYLVANIA

PLATE 52

COLONIAL INTERIORS, THIRD SERIES

Detail of Stair—1832

Hall and Stair—1832

CORSON HOUSE, PLYMOUTH MEETING, PENNSYLVANIA

Great Parlour. Panelling and all woodwork grained—c. 1690, c. 1725, c. 1830

SUNBURY HOUSE, CROYDON, BUCKS, PENNSYLVANIA

Parlour. Woodwork sage green, walls white—1684, c. 1710-1730

MARLPIT HALL, MIDDLETOWN, NEW JERSEY

Living Room—1731, 1770

BARTRAM HOUSE, KINGSESSING, PHILADELPHIA

PLATE 55

COLONIAL INTERIORS, THIRD SERIES

Living Room—1734

HANCOCK HOUSE, HANCOCK'S BRIDGE, SALEM COUNTY, NEW JERSEY

PLATE 56

Parlour—c. 1765

WASHINGTON'S HEADQUARTERS, VALLEY FORGE, PENNSYLVANIA

Parlour. Woodwork, pale green—1756

WOODFORD, FAIRMOUNT PARK, PHILADELPHIA

Parlour. Woodwork, pale green; coved cornice and ceiling white—1756

WOODFORD, FAIRMOUNT PARK, PHILADELPHIA

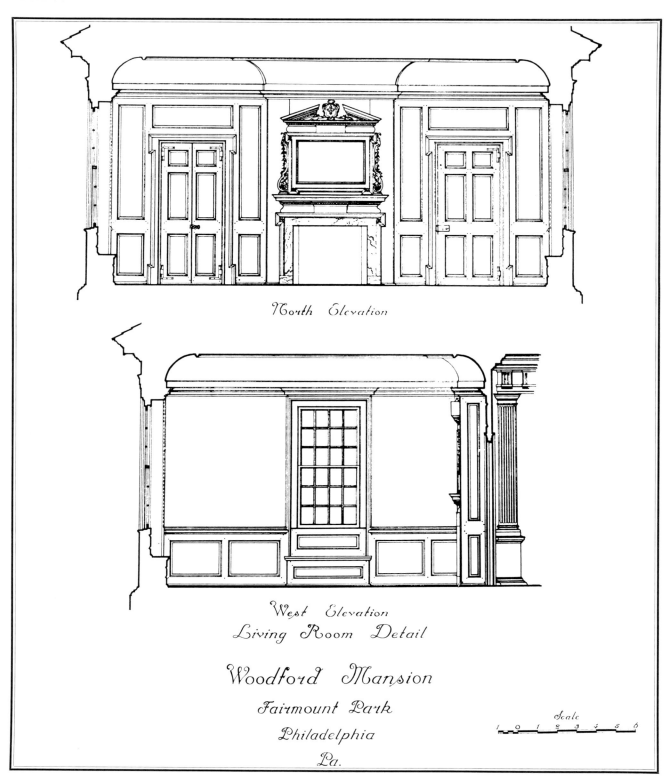

North Elevation

West Elevation
Living Room Detail

Woodford Mansion
Fairmount Park
Philadelphia
Pa.

Scale

(Upper) Sitting Room—1756
(Lower) Study (Old Kitchen)—1756

WOODFORD, FAIRMOUNT PARK, PHILADELPHIA

(Upper) West Parlour. Panelled walls and all woodwork white—1756
(Lower) East Parlour. Panelled walls and all woodwork green—1756

TULIP HILL, WEST RIVER, ANNE ARUNDEL COUNTY, MARYLAND

PLATE 61

COLONIAL INTERIORS, THIRD SERIES

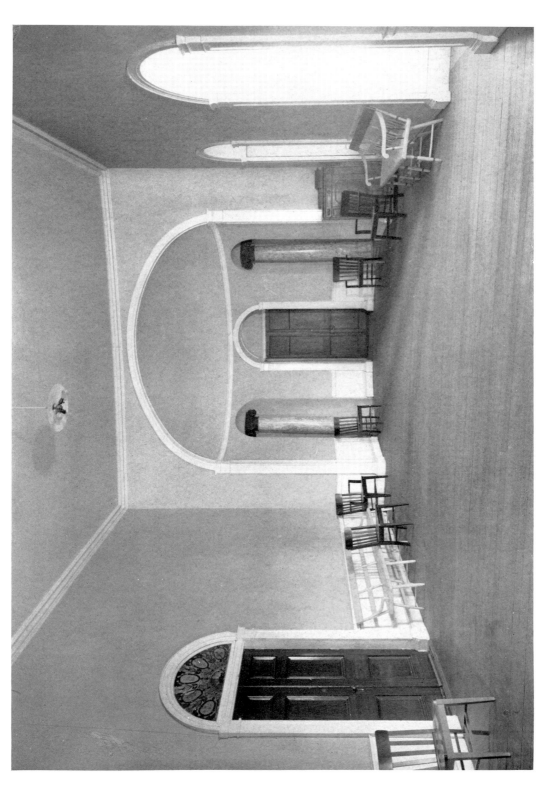

Ball Room. Woodwork white; walls grey—c. 1742, 1788

THE WOODLANDS, BLOCKLEY, PHILADELPHIA

PLATE 62

COLONIAL INTERIORS, THIRD SERIES

The salon with mantel designed by Thomas Jefferson. The two pier mirrors he brought with him from France. Over mantel is original painting of "Daughter of Herodias with the head of John the Baptist" brought by Jefferson from France—1769-1772

MONTICELLO, CHARLOTTESVILLE, VIRGINIA

Front Parlour. Woodwork white, curtains red damask—1798-1801

READ HOUSE, NEW CASTLE, DELAWARE

Parlour (in 1795 addition)—1721, 1752, 1795

CEDAR GROVE, FAIRMOUNT PARK, PHILADELPHIA (formerly at HARROGATE, PHILADELPHIA)

(Upper) Back Parlour, looking towards Front Parlour—1798-1801
(Lower) Front Parlour, looking towards Back Parlour. Woodwork in both rooms white—1798-1801

READ HOUSE, NEW CASTLE, DELAWARE

Parlour—1744, 1793,

PEN RHYN, CORNWELLS, PENNSYLVANIA

The "Psyche" Room—1744, 1793

PEN RYHN, CORNWELLS, PENNSYLVANIA

PLATE 66

COLONIAL INTERIORS, THIRD SERIES

Southeast Parlour—1797

SWEETBRIER, FAIRMOUNT PARK, PHILADELPHIA

PLATE 67

COLONIAL INTERIORS, THIRD SERIES

Northeast Parlour—1797

SWEETBRIER, FAIRMOUNT PARK, PHILADELPHIA

PLATE 68

COLONIAL INTERIORS, THIRD SERIES

Parlour (done over in 1824 before La Fayette's visit). Walls sea green; woodwork white, banded with pale green—1690, c. 1730, 1824

WYCK, GERMANTOWN, PHILADELPHIA

Old Parlour (1795).
  Walls, pale green; woodwork white. Curtains red, trimmed with yellow galons—c. 1750, 1795, 1830
ANDALUSIA, PENNSYLVANIA

Music Room (1827). Woodwork white, walls pale yellow.—1798, 1827
STRAWBERRY MANSION, FAIRMOUNT PARK, PHILADELPHIA

Music Room and Parlour—1798, 1827

STRAWBERRY MANSION, FAIRMOUNT PARK, PHILADELPHIA

Window opening from Old Parlour (1795) into Yellow Parlour (1830). Walls sea green; cornice and ceiling white; curtains red trimmed with gold figured galons. Door (1830) grained like curly maple— c. 1750, 1795, 1830

ANDALUSIA, PENNSYLVANIA

Yellow or Southwest Parlour (1830 addition)—c. 1750, 1795, 1830

ANDALUSIA, PENNSYLVANIA

Back Parlour. The modelled ornaments above doors and windows are in dull bronze; woodwork white. Walls pale Colonial yellow—1826

CADWALADER HOUSE (Mutual Assurance Co.), 240, SOUTH 4TH STREET, PHILADELPHIA

Southwest or Yellow Parlour, (1830). Walls pale Colonial yellow; woodwork white—c. 1750, 1795, 1830

ANDALUSIA, PENNSYLVANIA

PLATE 74

COLONIAL INTERIORS, THIRD SERIES

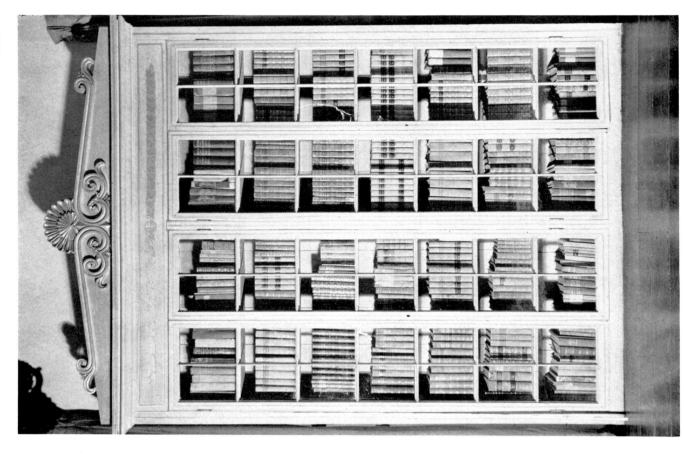

Library Bookcase. Fawn colour with gold decorations—c. 1750, 1795, 1830

ANDALUSIA, PENNSYLVANIA

Library (1830)—c. 1750, 1795, 1830

ANDALUSIA, PENNSYLVANIA

Library. Pale green walls, green woodwork. Grey veined marble mantel (1830)—1796, 1830

THE HIGHLANDS, WHITEMARSH VALLEY, PENNSYLVANIA

Library. Green woodwork, lighter green walls; Early Victorian carpet with brown ground, cream panels with polychrome flowers—1796, 1830

THE HIGHLANDS, WHITEMARSH VALLEY, PENNSYLVANIA

Parlour. Grey walls; white woodwork. Crimson curtains, gilded pelmets. Grey veined marble mantel (1830)—1796, 1830

THE HIGHLANDS, WHITEMARSH VALLEY, PENNSYLVANIA

(Upper) Parlour. Walls grey, curtains crimson, pelmets gilded, mantel grey veined marble. Early Victorian carpet with red ground. Much of the upholstery crimson—1796, 1830

THE HIGHLANDS, WHITEMARSH VALLEY, PENNSYLVANIA

(Lower) Parlour. The walls are dead white and always have been. White marble mantel c. 1810; glass chandelier also of about same date—1730, 1778, c. 1810

CLERMONT, LIVINGSTON MANOR, TIVOLI-ON-HUDSON, NEW YORK

PLATE 79

COLONIAL INTERIORS, THIRD SERIES

Parlour—c. 1832

GOVERNOUR'S HOUSE, NAVAL HOME, PHILADELPHIA

South and North Parlours. Walls pearl lavender; woodwork white—1836

OAKLAND HALL, OAKS, PENNSYLVANIA

North and South Parlours. Woodwork white; stiles and rails of doors light chocolate brown; mouldings white; fields of panels salmon—1760, 1835

HATFIELD HOUSE, FAIRMOUNT PARK, PHILADELPHIA

PLATE 81

COLONIAL INTERIORS, THIRD SERIES

Parlour—c. 1832

SEABURY TREDWELL HOUSE, 29, EAST 4TH ST., NEW YORK CITY

PLATE 82

COLONIAL INTERIORS, THIRD SERIES

Dining Room—1684, c. 1710-1730

MARLPIT HALL, MIDDLETOWN, NEW JERSEY

Dining Room (1721)—1721, 1752, 1795

CEDAR GROVE, FAIRMOUNT PARK, PHILADELPHIA (formerly at HARROGATE, PHILADELPHIA)

Dining Room (formerly Housekeeper's Room)—1756

TULIP HILL, WEST RIVER, ANNE ARUNDEL COUNTY, MARYLAND

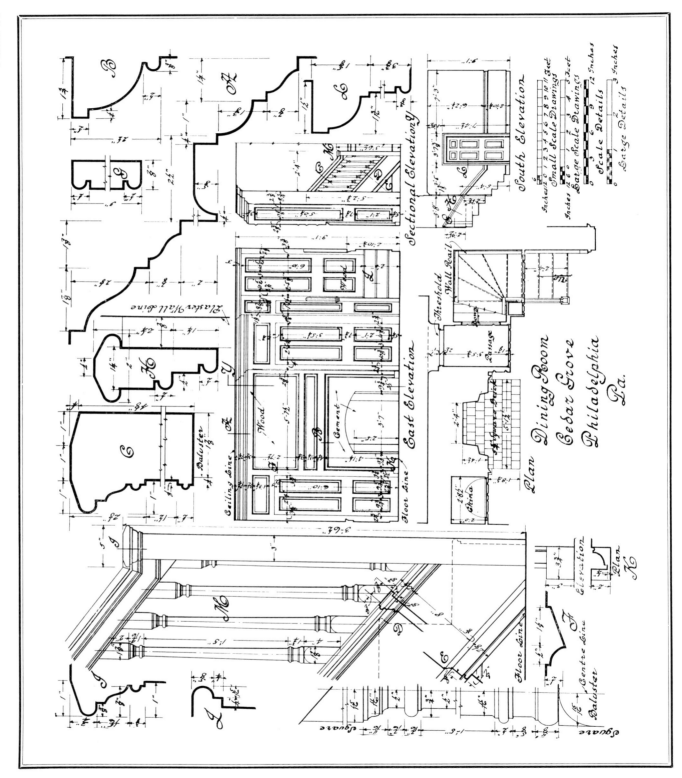

PLATE 84

COLONIAL INTERIORS, THIRD SERIES

South Elevation

Sectional Elevation

East Elevation

Plan Dining Room
Cedar Grove
Philadelphia
Pa.

PLATE 85

COLONIAL INTERIORS, THIRD SERIES

Dining Room Panelling and Fireplace—c. 1745

WHIPPOORWILL LODGE, RED BANK, NEW JERSEY

PLATE 86

COLONIAL INTERIORS, THIRD SERIES

Dining Room. Walls pale primrose yellow; woodwork white—1756

Fireplace in Dining Room—1756.

WOODFORD, FAIRMOUNT PARK, PHILADELPHIA

Fireplace in Bed Chamber. Woodwork sage green—1684, c. 1710-1730

MARLPIT HALL, MIDDLETOWN, NEW JERSEY

Fireplace and Panelling in Dining Room—c. 1765

WASHINGTON'S HEADQUARTERS, VALLEY FORGE, PENNSYLVANIA

PLATE 88

COLONIAL INTERIORS, THIRD SERIES

Dining Room—(1787)—1787, 1830

TODMORDEN HALL, WALLINGFORD, PENNSYLVANIA

PLATE 89

COLONIAL INTERIORS, THIRD SERIES

Breakfast Room—1769-1772

MONTICELLO, CHARLOTTESVILLE, VIRGINIA

Dining Room. White woodwork, yellow curtains—1798-1801

READ HOUSE, NEW CASTLE, DELAWARE

Dining Room. Polychrome painted paper—1798-1801

READ HOUSE, NEW CASTLE, DELAWARE

Dining Room. White woodwork, mahogany doors. Polychrome painted paper—-1798-1801

READ HOUSE, NEW CASTLE, DELAWARE

Great Northeast Chamber (1731). Walls and woodwork white—1731, 1770

BARTRAM HOUSE, KINGSESSING, PHILADELPHIA

Dining Room. Walls, pale primrose yellow. Mantel of black marble, c. 1810—1730, 1778, c. 1810

CLERMONT, LIVINGSTON MANOR, TIVOLI-ON-HUDSON, NEW YORK

PLATE 93

COLONIAL INTERIORS, THIRD SERIES

Banquet Room—1798, 1827

STRAWBERRY MANSION, FAIRMOUNT PARK,
PHILADELPHIA

Dining Room:—c. 1750, 1795, 1830

ANDALUSIA, PENNSYLVANIA

PLATE 94

COLONIAL INTERIORS, THIRD SERIES

Small Dining Room—1796, 1830

THE HIGHLANDS, WHITEMARSH VALLEY, PENNSYLVANIA

Glass Gallery—(1830).

PLATE 95

COLONIAL INTERIORS, THIRD SERIES

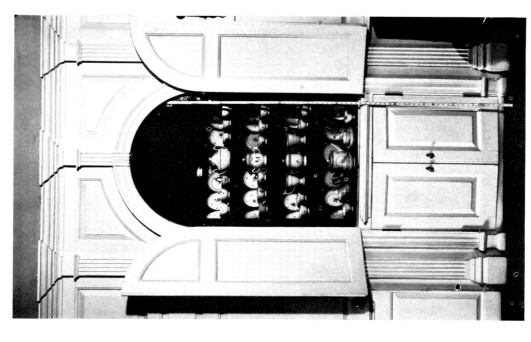

Corner Cupboard in Parlour—1684, c. 1710-1730

MARLPIT HALL, MIDDLETOWN,
NEW JERSEY

*Cupboard at end of Passage to North Wing
—1756*

TULIP HILL, WEST RIVER,
ANNE ARUNDEL COUNTY,
MARYLAND

Cupboard in Dining Room—c. 1745

WHIPPOORWILL LODGE, RED BANK
NEW JERSEY

PLATE 96

COLONIAL INTERIORS, THIRD SERIES

Canted Cupboard in Hall—1756

TULIP HILL, WEST RIVER, ANNE ARUNDEL COUNTY, MARYLAND

PLATE 97

COLONIAL INTERIORS, THIRD SERIES

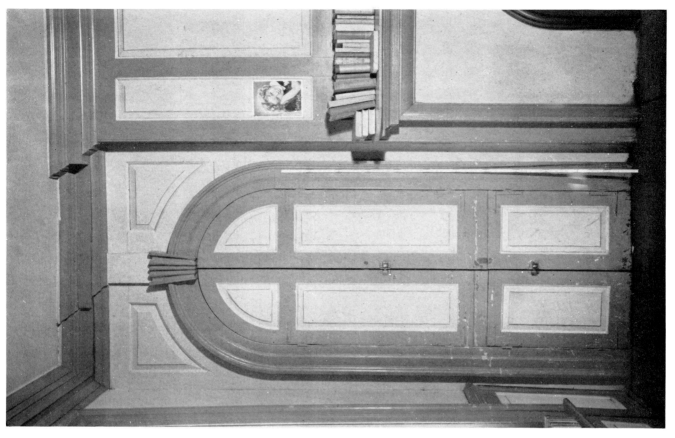

Cupboard and Panelling in Parlour—1765

LAUREL LODGE, POTTSTOWN

Cupboard in Great Chamber—1731, 1770

BARTRAM HOUSE, KINGSESSING, PHILADELPHIA

Bedroom. Woodwork sage green; walls white—1684, c. 1710-1730

MARLPIT HALL, MIDDLETOWN, NEW JERSEY

Bedroom—1756

WOODFORD, FAIRMOUNT PARK, PHILADELPHIA

West Bed Chamber and Canted Fireplace—1731, 1770

BARTRAM HOUSE, KINGSESSING, PHILADELPHIA

Bed Chamber—1734

HANCOCK HOUSE, HANCOCK'S BRIDGE, SALEM COUNTY, NEW JERSEY

Southeast Bed Chamber. Woodwork grey—c. 1740

TEUNIS DEY HOUSE, PREAKNESS, NEW JERSEY

Bed Chamber (formerly Ball Room). Woodwork sage green; walls lighter green—1756

WOODFORD, FAIRMOUNT PARK, PHILADELPHIA

East Bed Chamber—c. 1765

WASHINGTON'S HEADQUARTERS, VALLEY FORGE, PENNSYLVANIA

Bed Chamber (formerly Ball Room)—1756

WOODFORD, FAIRMOUNT PARK, PHILADELPHIA

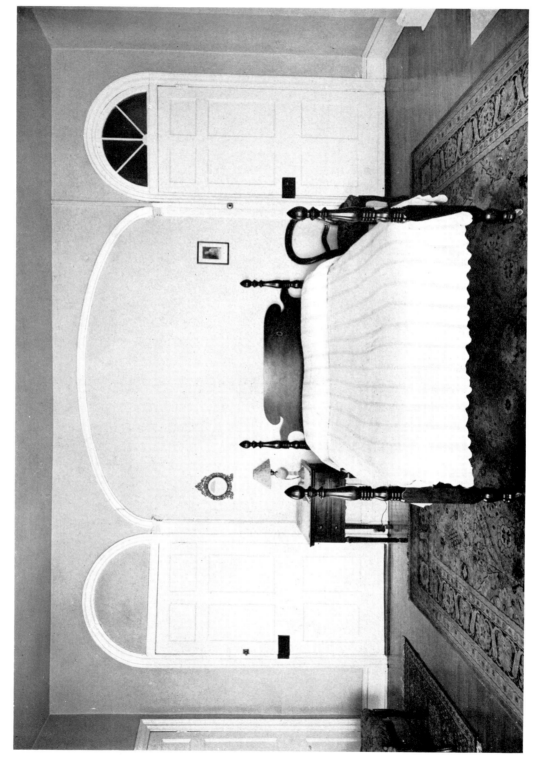

Northwest Bed Chamber with Bed Alcove (now closed)—c. 1742, 1788

THE WOODLANDS, BLOCKLEY, PHILADELPHIA

PLATE 103

COLONIAL INTERIORS, THIRD SERIES

An Alcove Bed in one of the second floor bedrooms—1769-1772

MONTICELLO, CHARLOTTESVILLE, VIRGINIA

PLATE 104

COLONIAL INTERIORS, THIRD SERIES

Bed Chamber—c. 1832

SEABURY TREDWELL HOUSE, 29, EAST 4TH ST., NEW YORK CITY

Kitchen Fireplace—1705

GENERAL VARNUM'S HEADQUARTERS, VALLEY FORGE, PENNSYLVANIA

Kitchen and Fireplace—1684, c. 1710-1730

MARLPIT HALL, MIDDLETOWN, NEW JERSEY

Kitchen fireplace, in Swedish portion of house, (c. 1645)—1731, 1770

BARTRAM HOUSE, KINGSESSING, PHILADELPHIA

Fireplace in present Dining Room (originally kitchen fireplace)—1740, c. 1810

CRESSBROOK FARM, VALLEY FORGE, PENNSYLVANIA

Fireplace in Kitchen—c. 1765

WASHINGTON'S HEADQUARTERS, VALLEY FORGE, PENNSYLVANIA

Kitchen (1795 part)—1721, 1752, 1795

CEDAR GROVE, FAIRMOUNT PARK, PHILADELPHIA (formerly at HARROGATE, PHILADELPHIA)

PLATE 108

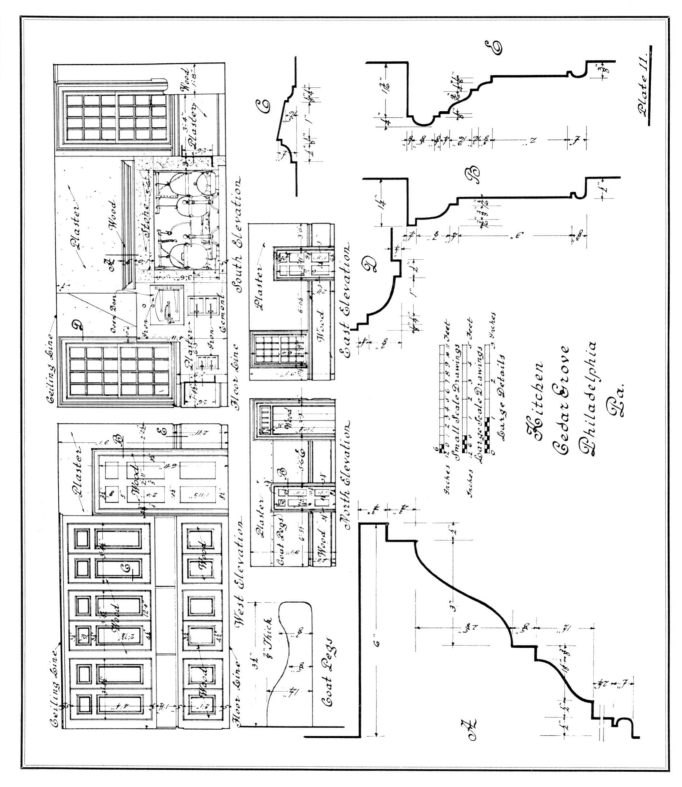

Kitchen
Cedar Grove
Philadelphia
Pa.

PLATE 109

COLONIAL INTERIORS, THIRD SERIES

Fireplace in Bed Chamber. Original colour of panelling and the boarding, vertical and horizontal, was sage green, with a landscape painted, c. 1728, on panel above fireplace. The whole now painted white and yellow—c. 1690, c. 1725, c. 1830

SUNBURY HOUSE, CROYDON, BUCKS, PENNSYLVANIA

Fireplace in Parlour. Sage green woodwork—1684, c. 1710-1730

MARLPIT HALL, MIDDLETOWN, NEW JERSEY

PLATE 110

COLONIAL INTERIORS, THIRD SERIES

Fireplace Detail, Southeast Bedroom. Grey woodwork—c. 1740

TEUNIS DEY HOUSE, PREAKNESS, NEW JERSEY

Fireplace Detail in Great Parlour. Grained woodwork—c. 1690, c. 1725, c. 1830

SUNBURY HOUSE, CROYDON, BUCKS, PENNSYLVANIA

PLATE 111

COLONIAL INTERIORS, THIRD SERIES

Fireplace, Panelling and Cupboard, East Bedroom—1719

Fireplace and Panelling, East Parlour—1719.

TRENT HOUSE, TRENTON, NEW JERSEY

PLATE 112

Fireplace in Southwest Parlour—1719

TRENT HOUSE, TRENTON, NEW JERSEY

PLATE 113

COLONIAL INTERIORS, THIRD SERIES

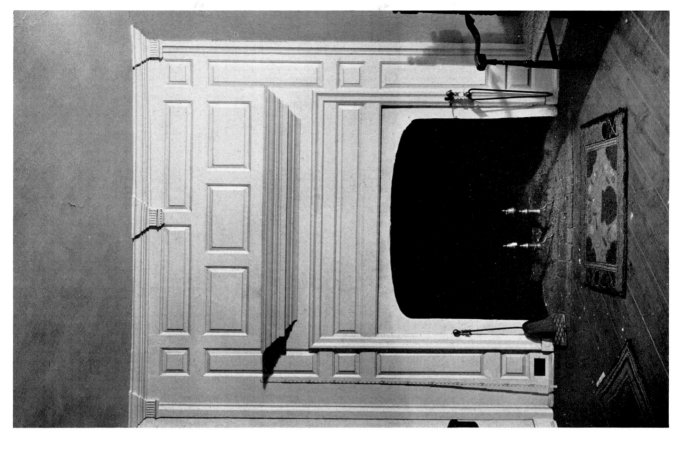

Parlour Fireplace—1727

ALEXANDER GRANT HOUSE, SALEM, NEW JERSEY

Bedroom Fireplace—1727

ALEXANDER GRANT HOUSE, SALEM, NEW JERSEY

PLATE 114

COLONIAL INTERIORS, THIRD SERIES

Fireplace in Bed Chamber—1705

GENERAL VARNUM'S HEADQUARTERS, VALLEY FORGE

Canted Fireplace in West Bed Chamber—1731, 1770

BARTRAM HOUSE, KINGSESSING, PHILADELPHIA

PLATE 115

COLONIAL INTERIORS, THIRD SERIES

Fireplace and Cupboard, Great Chamber—1731, 1770

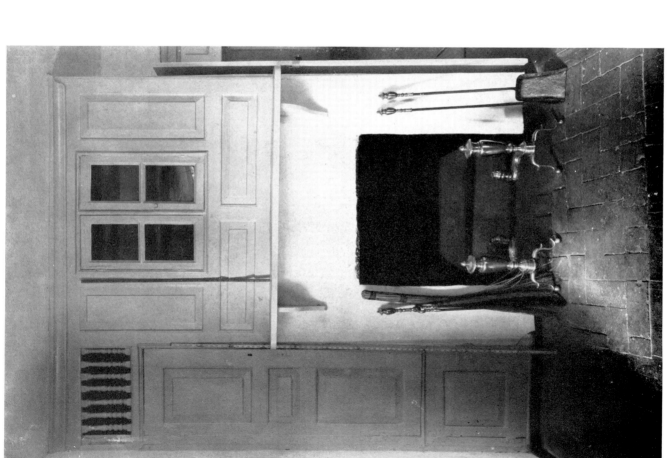

Fireplace and Cupboards in Living Room—1731, 1770.

BARTRAM HOUSE, KINGSESSING, PHILADELPHIA

Fireplace and Powder Closet, Bedroom—1734

HANCOCK HOUSE, HANCOCK'S BRIDGE, SALEM COUNTY, NEW JERSEY

Fireplace and Cupboard, Living Room—1734

HANCOCK HOUSE, HANCOCK'S BRIDGE, SALEM COUNTY, NEW JERSEY

PLATE 117

COLONIAL INTERIORS, THIRD SERIES

East Fireplace and Mantel in Dining Room (1740)—1740, c. 1810

CRESSBROOK FARM, VALLEY FORGE, PENNSYLVANIA

Fireplace, Panelling and Powder Closet in West Bedroom—1734

HANCOCK HOUSE, HANCOCK'S BRIDGE,
SALEM COUNTY, NEW JERSEY

Fireplace in Parlour—c. 1730, c. 1770

PINE FORGE HOUSE, PINE FORGE, PENNSYLVANIA

PLATE 119

COLONIAL INTERIORS, THIRD SERIES

Fireplace and Panelling in Ball Room—1750

THE INDIAN KING, HADDONFIELD, NEW JERSEY

PLATE 120

COLONIAL INTERIORS, THIRD SERIES

Door and Mantel Details, Dining Room—1756

Panelling and Mantel Detail, Bedroom (formerly Ball Room)—1756.

WOODFORD, FAIRMOUNT PARK, PHILADELPHIA

PLATE 121

COLONIAL INTERIORS, THIRD SERIES

Detail of Overmantel Carving—1756

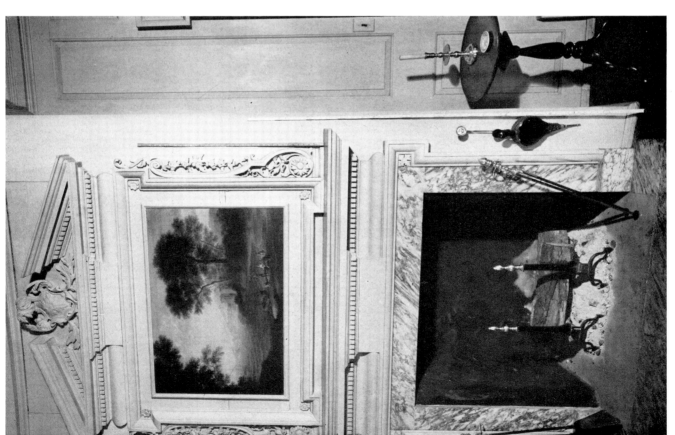

Fireplace and Overmantel, Parlour—1756.

WOODFORD, FAIRMOUNT PARK, PHILADELPHIA

PLATE 122

COLONIAL INTERIORS, THIRD SERIES

Mantel Detail, East Parlour—1756

Mantel Detail, West Parlour—1756.

TULIP HILL, WEST RIVER, ANNE ARUNDEL COUNTY, MARYLAND

PLATE 123

COLONIAL INTERIORS, THIRD SERIES

Detail of same—1765

Fireplace and Overmantel in Parlour—1765.

POWEL HOUSE, 244 SOUTH 3RD STREET, PHILADELPHIA

PLATE 124

COLONIAL INTERIORS, THIRD SERIES

Fireplace and Panelling, Parlour—c. 1765

Fireplace and Panelling, Southwest Bed Chamber—c. 1765.

WASHINGTON'S HEADQUARTERS, VALLEY FORGE, PENNSYLVANIA

PLATE 125

COLONIAL INTERIORS, THIRD SERIES

Fireplace in old Kitchen (now sitting-room). Woodwork sage green; walls white—1756

WOODFORD, FAIRMOUNT PARK, PHILADELPHIA

Fireplace and Panelling in Bedroom—1765. Paint recent

LAUREL LODGE, POTTSTOWN, PENNSYLVANIA

(Upper) Mantel in Southwest Bedroom—c. 1742, 1788
(Lower) Mantel in oval Drawing Room (now Dining Room). Black veined marble, with carved white marble ornament applied—c. 1742, 1788

THE WOODLANDS, BLOCKLEY, PHILADELPHIA

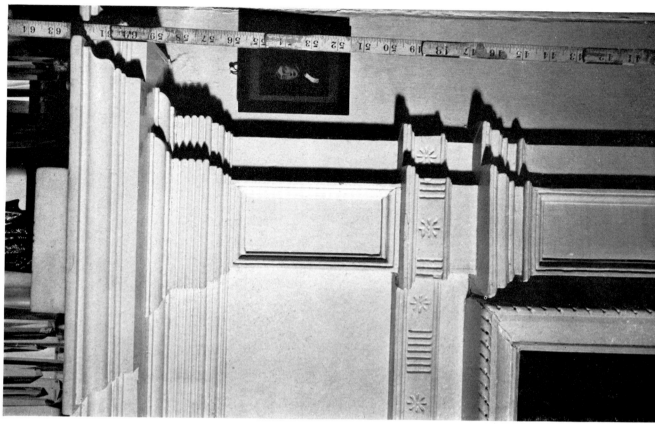

Detail of Mantel in Library (1790)—1687, 1790

BOLTON FARM, FALLSINGTON, BUCKS, PENNSYLVANIA

Detail of Mantel, Northeast Bedroom—c. 1742, 1788

THE WOODLANDS, BLOCKLEY, PHILADELPHIA

(Upper) Mantel in Northwest Bedroom—c. 1742, 1788
(Lower) Mantel in Southeast Bedroom—c. 1742, 1788

THE WOODLANDS, BLOCKLEY, PHILADELPHIA

PLATE 129

COLONIAL INTERIORS, THIRD SERIES

Elevation of Bedroom Fireplace

Scale in inches

Scale for details in inches

Details from Woodlands House of William Hamilton Philadelphia Pa.

PLATE 130

COLONIAL INTERIORS, THIRD SERIES

Mantel Detail in Bed Chamber—c. 1750

MASTER'S HOUSE, HEREFORD FURNACE, PENNSYLVANIA

Mantel Detail in Dining Room—1687, 1790

BOLTON FARM, FALLSINGTON, BUCKS, PENNSYLVANIA

(Upper) Mantel in Southwest Parlour—1807, c. 1850
(Lower) Mantel in Southwest Bedroom—1807, c. 1850

AULD HOUSE, RED BANK, NEW JERSEY (formerly on Long Island)

PLATE 132

COLONIAL INTERIORS, THIRD SERIES

Fireplace and Mantel, Northeast Parlour—1798-1801

UPSALA, GERMANTOWN, PHILADELPHIA

(Top Left) Mantel Detail, Northeast Parlour—1798-1801. (Top Right) Mantel Detail, Southeast Parlour—1798-1801. (Bottom) Mantel in Southeast Parlour—1798-1801

UPSALA, GERMANTOWN, PHILADELPHIA

(Upper) Fireplace and Mantel in Front Parlour. White woodwork, pale yellow walls—1798-1801
(Lower) Fireplace and Mantel in Back Parlour—1798-1801

READ HOUSE, NEW CASTLE, DELAWARE

PLATE 135

COLONIAL INTERIORS, THIRD SERIES

Parlour, Mantel, (c. 1810)—1730, 1778, c. 1810

CLERMONT, LIVINGSTON MANOR
TIVOLI-ON-HUDSON, NEW YORK

Detail of Mantel, Parlour—1798-1801

READ HOUSE
NEW CASTLE, DELAWARE

PLATE 136

COLONIAL INTERIORS, THIRD SERIES

Fireplace in Living Room (1810 addition)—1740, c. 1810

CRESSBROOK FARM, VALLEY FORGE, PENNSYLVANIA

Fireplace, North Parlour (Original Dining Room in 1798). Mantel, light sea green; walls, pale green—1798, 1827

STRAWBERRY MANSION, FAIRMOUNT PARK, PHILADELPHIA

Mantel in Reception Hall designed by Jefferson showing portrait after Rembrandt Peale—1769-1772

MONTICELLO, CHARLOTTESVILLE, VIRGINIA

PLATE 138

COLONIAL INTERIORS, THIRD SERIES

Detail of Mantel and Fireplace with hob grate in Dining Room (1795)— c. 1750, 1795, 1830

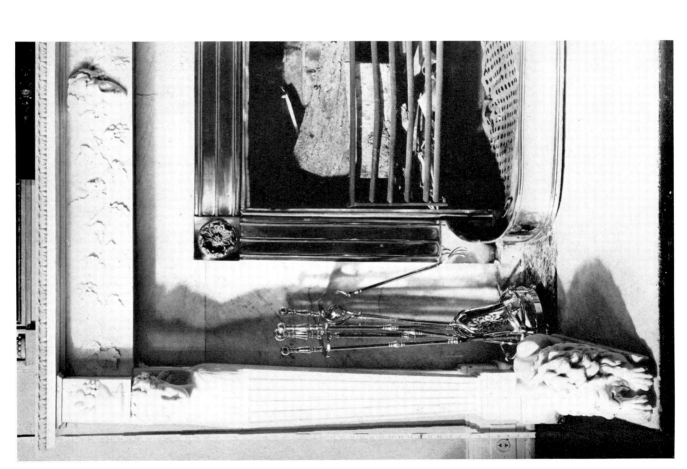

Detail of Mantel and Fireplace with hob grate in Old Parlour (1795).

ANDALUSIA, PENNSYLVANIA

PLATE 139

COLONIAL INTERIORS, THIRD SERIES

Mantel Detail in Back Parlour—1826

CADWALADER HOUSE (Mutual Assurance Co.), 240, SOUTH
4TH ST., PHILADELPHIA

Mantel Detail, Yellow Parlour—c. 1750, 1795, 1830

ANDALUSIA, PENNSYLVANIA

PLATE 140

COLONIAL INTERIORS, THIRD SERIES

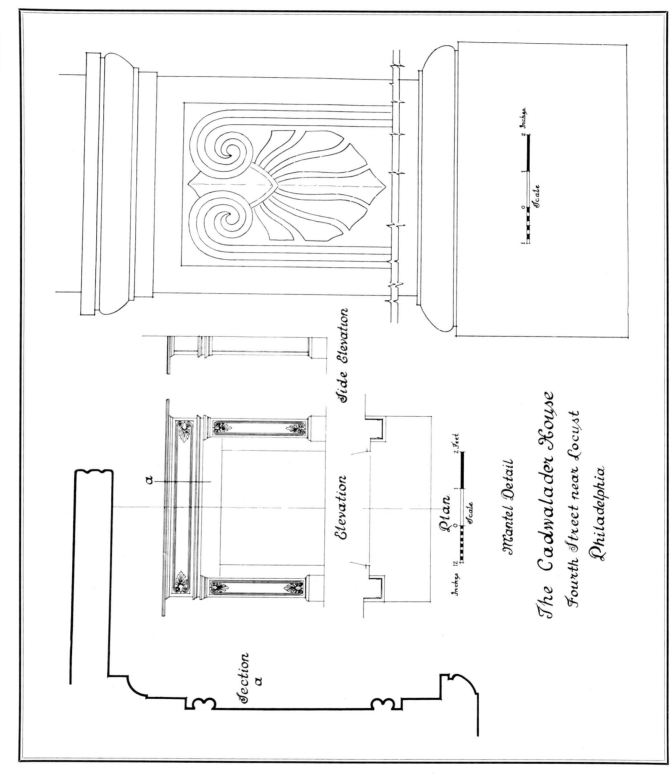

Section
a

Elevation

Side Elevation

Plan

Scale

Inches 12

2 Feet

Mantel Detail

The Cadwalader House
Fourth Street near Locust
Philadelphia

Scale

0

2 Inches

Fireplace and Mantel in Parlour—1812

GEORGE B. HOLLAND HOUSE, WALPOLE, NEW HAMPSHIRE

Mantel in North Parlour—1807, c. 1850

AULD HOUSE, RED BANK, NEW JERSEY (formerly on Long Island)

PLATE 142

COLONIAL INTERIORS, THIRD SERIES

Fireplace in Parlour (installed before La Fayette's visit in 1824)—1690, c. 1730, 1824

WYCK, GERMANTOWN, PHILADELPHIA

Panelling and Fireplace, Southwest Parlour—c. 1690, c. 1725, c. 1830

SUNBURY HOUSE, CROYDON, BUCKS, PENNSYLVANIA

PLATE 143

COLONIAL INTERIORS, THIRD SERIES

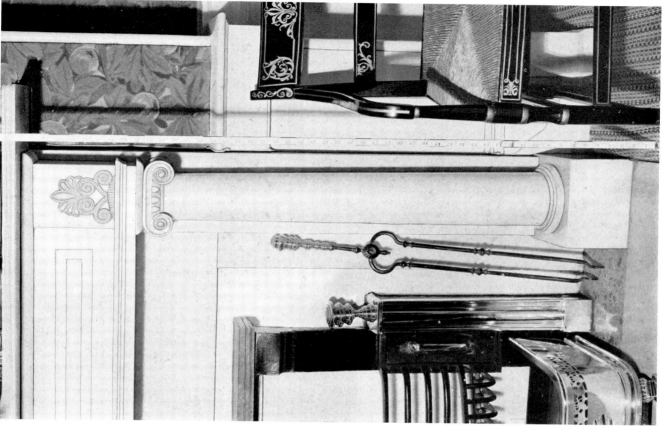

(Left) Dining Room. White marble mantel and hob grate (1830). Victorian Brussels carpet, tan, cream and dark red. (Right) Detail of same mantle —c. 1735, 1780, c. 1830

CARLTON, GERMANTOWN, PHILADELPHIA

Mantel in Dining Room (c. 1820)—1778

WAKEFIELD, PHILADELPHIA

Black veined marble Mantel, c. 1820

OAK HILL FARM, RED BANK, NEW JERSEY

Parlour Fireplace—1760, 1835

HATFIELD HOUSE, FAIRMOUNT PARK, PHILADELPHIA

PLATE 146

COLONIAL INTERIORS, THIRD SERIES

Window Detail in Ball Room. Woodwork white; walls pale yellow—1750

THE INDIAN KING, HADDONFIELD, NEW JERSEY

Window Detail in Parlour—1765

POWEL HOUSE, 244, SOUTH 3RD ST., PHILADELPHIA

PLATE 147

COLONIAL INTERIORS, THIRD SERIES

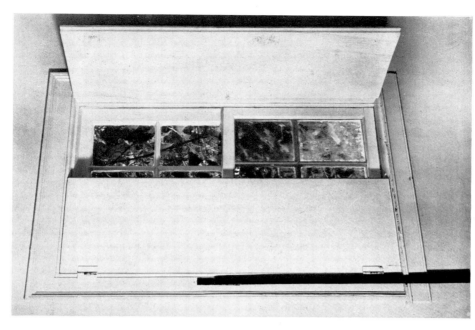

Window Detail in Passage to North Wing—1756

TULIP HILL, WEST RIVER, ANNE
ARUNDEL CO., MARYLAND

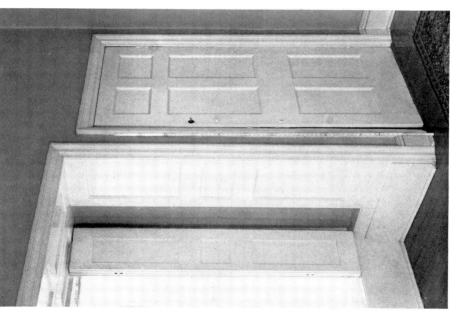

Bedroom Closet and Window Detail—c. 1742, 1788

THE WOODLANDS, BLOCKLEY
PHILADELPHIA

Upstairs Window Detail—1765

LAUREL LODGE, POTTSTOWN

PLATE 148

COLONIAL INTERIORS, THIRD SERIES

Window in Parlour. Woodwork white; stiles and rails of panelling beneath window, light chocolate brown; mouldings white; fields of panels salmon— 1760, 1835

HATFIELD HOUSE, FAIRMOUNT PARK, PHILADELPHIA

Window in Parlour—c. 1765

WASHINGTON'S HEADQUARTERS, VALLEY FORGE, PENNSYLVANIA

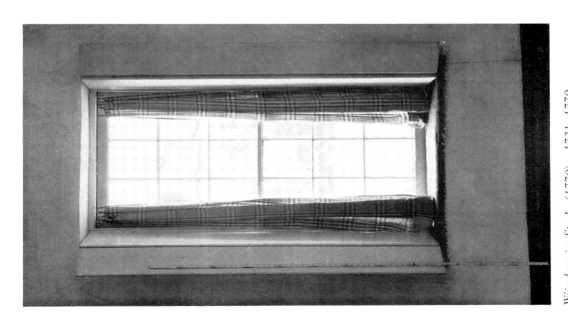

Window in Study (1770)—1731, 1770

BARTRAM HOUSE, BARTRAM'S GARDEN, KINGSESSING, PHILADELPHIA

PLATE 149

COLONIAL INTERIORS, THIRD SERIES

Palladian Window in upper Hall—1756

WOODFORD, FAIRMOUNT PARK, PHILADELPHIA

Palladian Window in upper Hall—1798-1801

READ HOUSE, NEW CASTLE, DELAWARE

PLATE 150

COLONIAL INTERIORS, THIRD SERIES

Panelling Detail beneath Bedroom Window (1830). Woodwork white—
c. 1735, 1780, c. 1830

CARLTON, GERMANTOWN, PHILADELPHIA

Heavy Latticed Door in Cellar—
1798-1801

READ HOUSE,
NEW CASTLE, DELAWARE

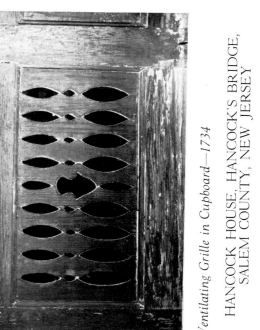

Ventilating Grille in Cupboard—1734

HANCOCK HOUSE, HANCOCK'S BRIDGE,
SALEM COUNTY, NEW JERSEY

Panelling Detail beneath Bedroom Window. Woodwork white—1798-1801

READ HOUSE, NEW CASTLE, DELAWARE

Plasterwork on Ceiling of Hall
Crossing—1798-1801

READ HOUSE,
NEW CASTLE, DELAWARE

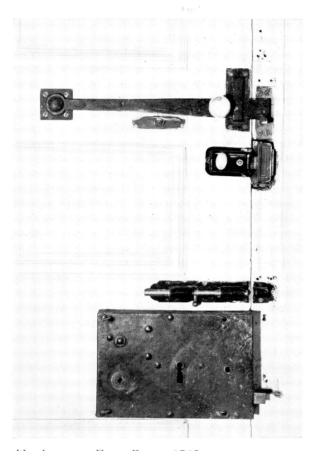

Hardware on Front Door—1765

POWEL HOUSE, 244, SOUTH 3RD ST.,
PHILADELPHIA

Hardware on House Door—1684, c. 1710-1730

MARLPIT HALL, MIDDLETOWN,
NEW JERSEY

Hardware on North Hall Door—c. 1735, 1780, c. 1830

CARLTON, GERMANTOWN,
PHILADELPHIA

Wrought Iron Hinge on Inside Door—1742

MORAVIAN *GEMEINHAUS*,
BETHLEHEM, PENNSYLVANIA

PLATE 152

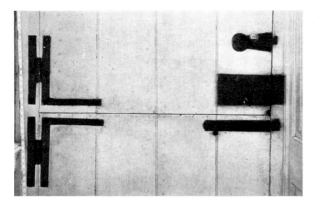

Hardware on Front Door—c. 1765

WASHINGTON'S HEADQUARTERS,
VALLEY FORGE, PENNSYLVANIA

Hardware inside of Front Door—1798-1801

UPSALA, GERMANTOWN,
PHILADELPHIA

Brass Hardware on Upstairs Door—1756

WOODFORD, FAIRMOUNT PARK,
PHILADELPHIA

Latch on Bedroom Door—c. 1690, c. 1725, c. 1830

SUNBURY HOUSE, CROYDON,
BUCKS, PENNSYLVANIA

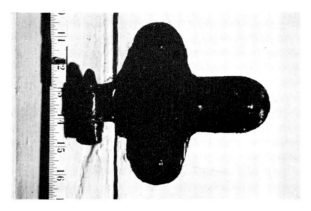

Wrought Iron Hinge—1742

MORAVIAN *GEMEINHAUS*,
BETHLEHEM, PENNSYLVANIA

Wooden Box Lock, Outer Door—1750

THE INDIAN KING, HADDONFIELD,
NEW JERSEY

PLATE 153

COLONIAL INTERIORS, THIRD SERIES

Wine Cellar in Basement—c. 1742, 1788

THE WOODLANDS, BLOCKLEY, PHILADELPHIA

JOHN F. OSBOURNE, INCORPORATED
BALTIMORE